❧

Presented to:

_____

By:

_____

Date:

_____

Occasion:

_____

The Joy of Believing Prayer
ISBN 1-57794-446-1
Copyright © 2001 by Joyce Meyer
Life In The Word, Inc.
P. O. Box 655
Fenton, Missouri 63026

Published by Harrison House, Inc.
P. O. Box 35035
Tulsa, Oklahoma 74153

THE JOY OF
BELIEVING PRAYER

Deepen Your Friendship With God

JOYCE MEYER

Harrison House

Contents

SIMPLE, BELIEVING PRAYER

*If we don't pray, the best
thing that can happen is
nothing, so that things will
stay the way they are,
which is frightening
enough in itself. We all
need change, and the way
to get it is through prayer.*

GOD'S WORD FOR YOU

And when you pray, do not heap up phrases (multiply words, repeating the same ones over and over) as the Gentiles do, for they think they will be heard for their much speaking. [I Kings 18:25-29.]

MATTHEW 6:7

one

SIMPLE, BELIEVING PRAYER

or many years I was dissatisfied with my prayer life. I was committed to praying every morning, but I always felt something was missing. I finally asked God what was wrong, and He responded in my heart by saying, "Joyce, you don't feel that your prayers are good enough." I was not enjoying prayer because I had no confidence that my prayers were acceptable.

Too often we get caught up in our own works concerning prayer. Sometimes we try to pray so long, loud, or fancy that we lose sight of the fact that prayer is simply conversation with God. The length or loudness or eloquence of our prayer is not the issue. It is the sincerity of our heart and the confidence that God hears and will answer us that is important.

We must develop the confidence that even if we simply say, "God help me," He hears and will answer. We can depend on God to be faithful to do what we have asked Him to do as long as our request is in accordance with His will. We should know that He wants to help us because He is our Helper (Hebrews 13:6).

Simple, believing prayer comes straight out of the heart and goes straight to the heart of God.

GOD'S WORD FOR YOU

Two men went up into the temple [enclosure] to pray, the one a Pharisee and the other a tax collector.

The Pharisee took his stand ostentatiously and began to pray thus before and with himself: God, I thank You that I am not like the rest of men—extortioners (robbers), swindlers [unrighteous in heart and life], adulterers—or even like this tax collector here.

I fast twice a week; I give tithes of all that I gain.

But the tax collector, [merely] standing at a distance, would not even lift up his eyes to heaven, but kept striking his breast, saying, O God, be favorable (be gracious, be merciful) to me, the especially wicked sinner that I am!

I tell you, this man went down to his home justified (forgiven and made upright and in right standing with God), rather than the other man; for everyone who exalts himself will be humbled, but he who humbles himself will be exalted.

LUKE 18:10-14

⟡

Humble Prayer

For prayer to be sincere, it must come from a humble heart. In this lesson on prayer taught by Jesus Himself, we see that the Pharisee prayed "ostentatiously," meaning that he prayed pretentiously, making an extravagant outward show. There was nothing secret or even sincere about his prayer. It even says that he prayed "before and with himself." In other words, his prayers never got two inches away from himself; he was all caught up in what *he* was doing.

The second man in the story, a despised tax collector and a "wicked sinner" in most people's eyes, humbled himself, bowed his head, and quietly, with humility, asked God to help him. In response to his sincere, humble prayer, a lifetime of sin was wiped away in a moment. This is the power of simple, believing prayer.

Build your faith on the fact that humble, believing prayer is powerful. Believe that you can pray anywhere, anytime, about anything. Believe that your prayers don't have to be perfect or eloquent or long. Keep them simple and full of faith.

We receive the grace of God by humbling ourselves
before Him, casting all our cares upon Him,
and trusting Him to take care of them
as He has promised in His Word.

GOD'S WORD FOR YOU

And I tell you, you are Peter [Greek, Petros—a large piece of rock], and on this rock [Greek, petra—a huge rock like Gibraltar] I will build My church, and the gates of Hades (the powers of the infernal region) shall not overpower it [or be strong to its detriment or hold out against it].

I will give you the keys of the kingdom of heaven; and whatever you bind (declare to be improper and unlawful) on earth must be what is already bound in heaven; and whatever you loose (declare lawful) on earth must be what is already loosed in heaven. [Isa. 22:22.]

MATTHEW 16:18-19

AUTHORITY THROUGH PRAYER

Since we are not only physical creatures but spiritual beings as well, we are able to stand in the physical realm and affect the spiritual realm. This is a very definite privilege and advantage. We can go into the spiritual realm through prayer and bring about action that will cause change in a situation. *God is a Spirit . . .* (John 4:24), and every answer we need to every situation is with Him.

Jesus told Peter that He would give him the keys of the Kingdom of heaven. Keys unlock doors, and I believe those keys (at least in part) can represent various types of prayer. Jesus went on to teach Peter about the power of binding and loosing, which operates on the same spiritual principle.

Jesus was also speaking to Peter about the power of faith in verse 18, and we know that one way faith is released is through prayer. The power of binding and loosing is also exercised in prayer.

When you and I pray about deliverance from some bondage in our lives or in the life of another, we are, in effect, binding that problem and loosing an answer. The act of prayer binds evil and looses good.

Jesus has conferred on us the power and authority to use the keys of the Kingdom to bring to pass the will of God on earth.

GOD'S WORD FOR YOU

Now Peter and John were going up to the temple at the hour of prayer. . . .

ACTS 3:1

❧

THE HABIT OF PRAYER

Many people feel vaguely guilty about their prayer life because they compare themselves to others. God is a creative God and wants each person to have his or her own individual prayer life. It doesn't have to be just like that of anyone else.

Yes, there are definite principles of prayer that need to be followed. As we see here in the book of Acts, the early disciples set aside certain hours of the day when they would go to a designated place to pray. That is good self-discipline, but that should be the start of prayer and not the finish. We should discipline ourselves to establish a prayer schedule that is individually suited to us and then stick to it until it becomes such a part of our lifestyle that we do it without even thinking.

All day we can continue to communicate with the Lord, praising and worshiping Him, thanking Him for His presence with us and asking His help in all our problems. Then just before we go to sleep at night, we can offer up a final prayer of gratitude for the blessings of the day and a request for a peaceful and refreshing night's sleep.

God wants prayer to be a normal part of our lives.

GOD'S WORD FOR YOU

Be unceasing in prayer [praying perseveringly].

1 THESSALONIANS 5:17

∽◈∾

Pray at all times (on every occasion, in every season) in the Spirit, with all [manner of] prayer and entreaty. To that end keep alert and watch with strong purpose and perseverance, interceding in behalf of all the saints (God's consecrated people).

EPHESIANS 6:18

∽◈∾

PRAY WITHOUT CEASING

The *King James Version* of this verse says, "Pray without ceasing."

I used to wonder, *Lord, how can I ever get to the place that I am able to pray without ceasing?* To me the phrase "without ceasing" meant nonstop, without ever quitting. I couldn't see how that was possible.

Now I have a better understanding of what Paul was saying. He meant that prayer should be like breathing, something we do continually but often unconsciously. Our physical bodies require breathing. Likewise, our spiritual bodies are designed to be nurtured and sustained by continual prayer.

The problem is that because of religious thinking we have the mistaken idea that if we don't keep up a certain schedule of prayer we are missing the mark. If we become too "religious" about prayer, thinking we must do it one way or the other because that is how someone else does it, we will bring condemnation on ourselves. The important lesson about prayer is not the posture or the time or place but learning to pray in faith—at all times, unceasingly.

❧

It is the Holy Spirit Who will lead you into prayer without ceasing.

GOD'S WORD FOR YOU

Do not fret or have any anxiety about anything, but in every circumstance and in everything, by prayer and petition (definite requests), with thanksgiving, continue to make your wants known to God.

And God's peace [shall be yours, that tranquil state of a soul assured of its salvation through Christ, and so fearing nothing from God and being content with its earthly lot of whatever sort that is, that peace] which transcends all understanding shall garrison and mount guard over your hearts and minds in Christ Jesus.

PHILIPPIANS 4:6-7

PRAYER PRODUCES PEACE

In this passage the apostle Paul does not say, "Pray and worry." Instead, he says, "Pray and don't worry." Why are we to pray and not worry? Because prayer is supposed to be the way we *cast our care* upon the Lord.

When the devil tries to give us care, we are supposed to turn and give that care to God. That's what prayer is, our acknowledgment to the Lord that we cannot carry our burden of care, so we lay it all on Him. If we pray about something and then keep on worrying about it, we are mixing a positive and a negative. The two cancel each other out so that we end up right back where we started—at zero.

Prayer is a positive force; worry is a negative force. The Lord has told me the reason many people operate at zero power level spiritually is that they cancel out their positive prayer power by giving in to the negative power of worry.

As long as we are worrying, we are not trusting God. It is only by trusting, by having faith and confidence in the Lord, that we are able to enter into His rest and enjoy the peace that transcends all understanding.

Make a decision now to cast all your care on the Lord and begin to watch Him take care of you.

GOD'S WORD FOR YOU

Come to Me, all you who labor and are heavy-laden and overburdened, and I will cause you to rest. [I will ease and relieve and refresh your souls.]

Take My yoke upon you and learn of Me, for I am gentle (meek) and humble (lowly) in heart, and you will find rest (relief and ease and refreshment and recreation and blessed quiet) for your souls.

MATTHEW 11:28-29

For we who have believed [adhered to and trusted in and relied on God) do enter that rest.

HEBREWS 4:3

PRAYER PRODUCES REST

If we are not at rest, we are not believing, because the fruit of believing is rest.

For many years of my life I would claim, "Oh, I'm believing God; I'm trusting the Lord." But I was not doing either of those things. I didn't know the first thing about believing God or trusting the Lord. I was anxious, panicky, irritable, and on edge all the time.

Just as we can be involved in outward activity, we can be involved in inward activity. God wants us not only to enter into His rest in our body, He also wants us to enter into His rest in our soul.

To me, finding rest, relief, ease, refreshment, recreation, and blessed quiet for my soul means finding freedom from mental activity. It means not having to live in the torment of reasoning, always trying to come up with an answer I don't have. I don't have to worry; instead, I can remain in a place of quiet peace and rest through prayer.

If we are truly believing God and trusting the Lord, we have entered into His rest. We have prayed and cast our care upon Him and are now abiding in the perfect peace of His holy presence.

You can speak His Word to your raging soul and tortured mind just as Jesus spoke to the wind and waves and said, "Peace, be still."

GOD'S WORD FOR YOU

Through Him also we have [our] access (entrance, introduction) by faith into this grace (state of God's favor) in which we [firmly and safely] stand. And let us rejoice and exult in our hope of experiencing and enjoying the glory of God.

Moreover [let us also be full of joy now!] let us exult and triumph in our troubles and rejoice in our sufferings, knowing that pressure and affliction and hardship produce patient and unswerving endurance.

And endurance (fortitude) develops maturity of character (approved faith and tried integrity). And character [of this sort] produces [the habit of] joyful and confident hope.

ROMANS 5:2-4

PRAYER PRODUCES PATIENCE AND HOPE

It is easy to say, "Don't worry." But to actually do that requires experience with God. I don't think there is any way a person can fully overcome the habit of worry, anxiety, and fear and develop the habit of peace, rest, and hope without years of experience.

That's why it is so important to continue to have faith and trust in God in the very midst of trials and tribulations. We must steadfastly resist the temptation to give up and quit when the going gets rough—and keeps on getting rougher over a long period of time. It is in those hard, trying times that the Lord is building in us the patience, endurance, and character that will eventually produce the habit of joyful and confident hope.

When you and I are in the midst of battle against our spiritual enemy, every round we go through produces valuable experience and strength. Each time we endure an attack, we become stronger. If we hang in there and refuse to give up, sooner or later we will be more than the devil can handle. When that happens, we will have reached spiritual maturity.

*We serve a God Who is so marvelous
that He can work out things for our good
that Satan intends for our harm.*

GOD'S WORD FOR YOU

All of these with their minds in full agreement devoted themselves steadfastly to prayer.

ACTS 1:14

UNITED OR CORPORATE PRAYER

Whenever believers are united in corporate prayer, there is great power present. Jesus Himself said, "For wherever two or three are gathered (drawn together as My followers) in (into) My name, there I AM in the midst of them" (Matthew 18:20).

Throughout the book of Acts we read that the people of God came together "with one accord" (Acts 2:1, 46; 4:24; 5:12; 15:25 KJV). And it was their united faith, their corporate agreement, and the presence of Jesus by the power of the Holy Spirit that made their prayers so effective. They saw God move in mighty ways to confirm the truth of His Word as they gave testimony to their faith in Jesus.

Then in Philippians 2:2 we are told by the apostle Paul, "Fill up and complete my joy by living in harmony and being of the same mind and one in purpose, having the same love, being in full accord and of one harmonious mind and intention."

Paul is giving us an important principle about corporate prayer. If we will heed these words and come into harmony and agreement with one another and with God, we will experience the same kind of powerful results the first-century disciples enjoyed in the book of Acts.

When you come together to pray,
expect God to show His power!

GOD'S WORD FOR YOU

And the Lord said to Moses, I have seen this people, and behold, it is a stiff-necked people;

Now therefore let Me alone, that My wrath may burn hot against them and that I may destroy them; but I will make of you a great nation.

But Moses besought the Lord his God, and said, Lord, why does Your wrath blaze hot against Your people, whom You have brought forth out of the land of Egypt with great power and a mighty hand?

[Earnestly] remember Abraham, Isaac, and Israel, Your servants, to whom You swore by Your own self and said to them, I will multiply your seed as the stars of the heavens, and all this land that I have spoken of will I give to your seed, and they shall inherit it forever.

Then the Lord turned from the evil which He had thought to do to His people.

EXODUS 32:9-11, 13-14

GOD CHANGES PEOPLE THROUGH PRAYER

Moses' intercession for the children of Israel is a stirring example that depicts how sincere prayer can change God's mind.

There are times when I can sense that God is getting weary of putting up with someone who is not obeying Him, and I will find myself being led to pray for God to be merciful to that person and to give that individual another chance.

As Jesus told His disciples at Gethsemane, we should "watch and pray" (Matthew 26:41 KJV). We need to pray for one another, not judge and criticize each other. If we watch people, we can see when they need encouragement, when they are depressed, fearful, insecure, or experiencing any number of obvious problems. God allows us to discern their need in order to be part of the answer, not part of the problem. Remember we are not the potter. God is, and we certainly don't know how to "fix" people.

People who are hurting don't need someone with a spirit of pride trying to *fix* them; they need acceptance, love, and prayer.

Pray! Pray! Pray! It is the only way to get things accomplished in God's economy. If we do things His way, we always get good results.

We need to do the praying and let God do the working.

GOD'S WORD FOR YOU

For we are fellow workmen (joint promoters, laborers together) with and for God; you are God's garden and vineyard and field under cultivation, [you are] God's building.

1 CORINTHIANS 3:9

Do you not discern and understand that you [the whole church at Corinth] are God's temple (His sanctuary), and that God's Spirit has His permanent dwelling in you [to be at home in you, collectively as a church and also individually]?

1 CORINTHIANS 3:16

WE ARE THE PLACE OF PRAYER

Under the Old Covenant, the temple was the house of God, the place of prayer for His people, the children of Israel. And no expense was spared to beautify the temple where the people came to worship the Lord their God. In 1 Kings 6 we have a description of Solomon's temple, which contained the ark of the covenant, God's pledge of His presence.

Under the New Covenant the apostle Paul instructs us that God's presence is now a mystery revealed of Christ in us, "the Hope of glory" (Colossians 1:27). Because of the union we now have in Christ, we are God's living temple. We are indwelt by the Holy Spirit, a building still under construction, but nonetheless His house, His tabernacle. That is why Paul goes to great length to tell us to live a holy life. We are a temple of the living God.

Whereas the children of Israel had to go to a specific place to offer their worship with detailed instructions, we have the incredible privilege of worshiping God anywhere and at any time. Therefore, we should be called a house of prayer.

We become the sanctuary of God because of the presence of the Holy One in us.

How to Pray Effectively

*There is nothing more powerful
to change our lives and
the lives of those around us
than God's hand moving in response
to our heartfelt, continued prayer.*

GOD'S WORD FOR YOU

The earnest (heartfelt, continued) prayer of a righteous man makes tremendous power available [dynamic in its working].

JAMES 5:16

t w o

HOW TO PRAY EFFECTIVELY

 reached a point in my prayer life where I felt frustrated, so I began to seek God about it. I wanted the assurance that "the earnest, heartfelt prayer of a righteous man makes tremendous power available, dynamic in its working." I wanted God's power made available to change that situation or bless that person's life over which I was praying.

If we're going to learn how to pray effectively, we have to say, "Lord, teach me to pray." He will show you the keys to praying more effectively. Keys lock and unlock. Keys reflect authority. Whoever has the keys has the authority. When we pray this way, we're asking the Lord to reveal His prayer principles that will make our prayers effective.

I encourage you to start seeking God's will when you pray, because there will be an anointing on prayer that is in line with His will. God showed me that to pray fervently means to put your whole self, all of your attention, your mind, your will, your emotions, all of you into what you're praying about. He is more concerned with the quality of prayer than the quantity of prayer.

Be shamelessly persistent in prayer.

GOD'S WORD FOR YOU

The effective, fervent prayer of a righteous man avails much.

JAMES 5:16 NKJV

∽✕∾

The heartfelt supplication of a righteous man exerts a mighty influence.

JAMES 5:16 WEYMOUTH

∽✕∾

. . . The prayers of the righteous have a powerful effect.

JAMES 5:16 MOFFATT

∽✕∾

FERVENT PRAYER

For prayer to be effective it must be fervent. However, if we misunderstand the word *fervent*, we may feel that we have to "work up" some strong emotion before we pray; otherwise, our prayers will not be effective.

I know there were many years when I believed this way, and perhaps you have been likewise confused or deceived. Look at some of the other translations of this verse that may make its meaning clearer: "fervent prayer . . . avails much"; "exerts a mighty influence"; "have a powerful effect."

I believe this scripture means that our prayers must come out of our heart and not just our head.

At times I experience a great deal of emotion while at prayer. Sometimes I even cry. But there are plenty of times when I don't feel emotional. Believing prayer is not possible if we base the value of our prayers on feelings. I remember enjoying so much those prayer times when I could *feel* God's presence, and then wondering what was wrong during the times when I didn't *feel* anything. I learned after a while that faith is not based on *feelings* in the emotions but on knowledge in the heart.

Trust that your earnest, heartfelt prayers are effectual because your faith is in Him, not in your own ability to live holy or pray eloquently.

GOD'S WORD FOR YOU

. . . The effective, fervent prayer of a righteous man avails much.

Elijah was a man with a nature like ours, and he prayed earnestly that it would not rain; and it did not rain on the land for three years and six months.

JAMES 5:16-17

THE PRAYERS OF A RIGHTEOUS MAN

James tells us that the fervent prayer of a "righteous" man is powerful. This means a man who is not under condemnation—one who has confidence in God and in the power of prayer. It does not mean a man without any imperfection in his life.

Elijah was a man of God who did not always behave perfectly, but he did not allow his imperfections to steal his confidence in God. Elijah had faith, but he also had fear. He was obedient, but at times he was also disobedient. He loved God and wanted to fulfill His will and calling upon his life. But sometimes he gave in to human weaknesses and tried to avoid the consequences of that will and calling.

In 1 Kings 18 we see him moving in tremendous power, calling down fire from heaven and slaying 450 prophets of Baal. Then immediately we see him fearfully running from Jezebel, becoming negative and depressed, and even wanting to die.

Like many of us, Elijah let his emotions get the upper hand. He was a human being just like us, and yet he prayed powerful prayers. His example should give us enough "scriptural power" to defeat condemnation when it rises up to tell us we cannot pray powerfully because of our weaknesses and faults.

Never underestimate the power
of effective, fervent prayer!

GOD'S WORD FOR YOU

And when you pray, do not keep on babbling like pagans, for they think they will be heard because of their many words. Do not be like them, for your Father knows what you need before you ask him.

MATTHEW 6:7-8 NIV

SHORT AND SIMPLE

I believe God has instructed me to pray and make my requests with as few words as possible. If I can keep my request very simple and not confuse the issue by trying to come up with too many words, my prayer actually seems to be more clear and powerful.

We need to spend our energy releasing our faith, not repeating phrases over and over that only serve to make the prayer long and involved.

It has actually been difficult for me to keep my prayers short and simple. I began to realize that my problem in praying was that I didn't have faith that my prayer would get through if it was short, simple, and to the point. I had fallen into the same trap that many people do—"the-longer-the-better" mentality. I don't mean that I am advocating praying only for a short period of time, but I am suggesting that each prayer be simple, direct, to the point, and filled with faith.

Now as I follow God's direction to keep it simple and make my request with the least amount of words possible, I experience a much greater release of my faith, and I know that God has heard me and will answer.

If your prayers are complicated, simplify them.
If you are not praying enough, pray more.

GOD'S WORD FOR YOU

Keep on asking and it will be given you; keep on seeking and you will find; keep on knocking [reverently] and [the door] will be opened to you.

For everyone who keeps on asking receives; and he who keeps on seeking finds; and to him who keeps on knocking, [the door] will be opened.

MATTHEW 7:7-8

How Many Times Should I Pray?

I don't believe we can make any strict rules on the subject of how often to pray about the same thing. I do think there are some guidelines that may apply to help us have even more confidence in the power of prayer.

If my children need something, I would want them to trust me to do what they asked me to do. I wouldn't mind, and might even like it, if they occasionally said, "Boy, Mom, I'm sure looking forward to those new shoes." That statement would declare to me that they believed I was going to do what I promised. They would actually be reminding me of my promise, but in a way that would not question my integrity.

I believe sometimes when we ask God the same thing over and over, it is a sign of doubt and unbelief, not of faith and persistence.

When I ask the Lord for something in prayer, and that request comes to my mind later, I talk to Him about it again. But when I do, I refrain from asking Him the same thing as if I think He didn't hear me the first time. I thank the Lord that He is working on the situation I prayed about previously.

Faithful, persistent prayer builds even more faith and confidence in us as we continue to pray.

GOD'S WORD FOR YOU

And this is the confidence (the assurance, the privilege of boldness) which we have in Him: [we are sure] that if we ask anything (make any request) according to His will (in agreement with His own plan), He listens to and hears us.

And if (since) we [positively] know that He listens to us in whatever we ask, we also know [with settled and absolute knowledge] that we have [granted us as our present possessions] the requests made of Him.

1 JOHN 5:14-15

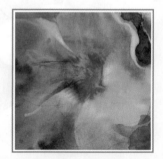

BELIEVE GOD HEARS YOU!

When you pray, believe God hears you!

In John 11:41-42, just before Jesus called Lazarus forth from the tomb, Jesus prayed: "Father, I thank You that You have heard Me. Yes, I know You always hear and listen to Me, but I have said this on account of and for the benefit of the people standing around, so that they may believe that You did send Me [that You have made Me Your Messenger]." What confidence!

Satan does not want us to have that kind of confidence either. But I encourage you one more time: *Be confident!* Make a decision that you are a believer, not a beggar. Go to the throne in Jesus' name—His name will get attention!

Because my ministry is broadcast on TV, a few people know who I am, and some people like to use my name. My employees like to say, "I work for Joyce Meyer," and my children like to say, "Joyce Meyer is my mother." They think those they are approaching may give them more favor if they mention my name.

If that works for us as human beings, just think how well it must work in the heavenly realm— especially when we use the name that is above all other names—the blessed name of Jesus! (Philippians 2:9-11).

Go to God in prayer—boldly. With confidence. In the name of Jesus.

GOD'S WORD FOR YOU

Then He was praying in a certain place; and when He stopped, one of His disciples said to Him, Lord, teach us to pray, [just] as John taught his disciples.

And He said to them, When you pray, say: Our Father Who is in heaven, hallowed be Your name, Your kingdom come. Your will be done [held holy and revered] on earth as it is in heaven.

Give us daily our bread [food for the morrow].

And forgive us our sins, for we ourselves also forgive everyone who is indebted to us [who has offended us or done us wrong]. And bring us not into temptation but rescue us from evil.

LUKE 11:1-4

KNOW GOD AS YOUR FATHER

For many years I prayed the "Lord's Prayer," and I no more knew God as my Father than anything! I didn't have any kind of a close personal relationship with God. I was just repeating something I had learned.

If you want to be effective in your prayer life, you need to know God as your Father. When the disciples asked Jesus to teach them to pray, He taught them what we call the "Lord's Prayer," which is a spiritual treasure house of principles for prayer. But foremost, Jesus started out by instructing them to say, "Our Father Who is in heaven, hallowed be Your name."

Jesus was showing them the importance of seeing the privileged relationship He came to bring to every believer. He told them they needed to have a relationship with God as their Father if they expected to go to Him in prayer. Don't go to God as some ogre that you're afraid of, but develop a Father-child relationship with Him. That intimate relationship will give you liberty to ask Him for things you would not have asked for if you had a starchy, stiff relationship with Him.

Our heavenly Father longs to give good gifts to His children.

When you pray, remember you have a loving Father Who is listening.

GOD'S WORD FOR YOU

And He said to them, Which of you who has a friend will go to him at midnight and will say to him, Friend, lend me three loaves [of bread],

For a friend of mine who is on a journey has just come, and I have nothing to put before him;

And he from within will answer, Do not disturb me; the door is now closed, and my children are with me in the bed; I cannot get up and supply you [with anything]?

I tell you, although he will not get up and supply him anything because he is his friend, yet because of his shameless persistence and insistence he will get up and give him as much as he needs.

LUKE 11:5-8

BECOME A FRIEND OF GOD

The key to this scripture is *friendship*. The man in the story went at midnight to get bread for his friend in need. If the person you're going to isn't your friend, you will not shamelessly persist. Jesus was telling His disciples that God is much more willing to give us what we need than the man in the parable was to give to his friend.

Jesus said, "You are My friends if you keep on doing the things which I command you to do" (John 15:14). We're talking about a right heart attitude, that you're going to obey God no matter what it costs you. That's one of the criteria for being a friend of God. You also become His friend because you spend a lot of time with Him.

Isaiah 41:8 says, "But you, Israel, My servant, Jacob, whom I have chosen, the offspring of Abraham My friend." What an awesome thing to have God call you His friend. When God was going to bring judgment, He said, "Shall I hide from Abraham [My friend and servant] what I am going to do. . . ?" (Genesis 18:7). And as His friend, you can expect to have firsthand knowledge about what God is doing.

*The closer friend you become with God,
the more boldness you have when you pray.*

GOD'S WORD FOR YOU

Let us then fearlessly and confidently and boldly draw near to the throne of grace (the throne of God's unmerited favor to us sinners), that we may receive mercy [for our failures] and find grace to help in good time for every need [appropriate help and well-timed help, coming just when we need it].

HEBREWS 4:16

BE BOLD!

When you and I pray, we need to make sure we approach God as believers, not as beggars. Remember, according to Hebrews 4:16, we are to come boldly to the throne: not beggarly, but boldly; not belligerently, but boldly.

Be sure to keep the balance. Stay respectful, but be bold. Approach God with confidence. Believe He delights in your prayers and is ready to answer any request that is in accordance with His will.

As believers, we should know the Word of God, which is His will; therefore, it should be easy for us to pray according to God's will. Don't approach God wondering if what you are asking is His will. Settle that issue in your heart *before* you pray.

As you and I come boldly before the throne of God's grace, covered with the blood of Jesus, asking in faith according to His Word and in the name of His Son Jesus Christ, we can know that we have the petitions that we ask of Him. Not because we are perfect or worthy of ourselves, or because God owes us anything, but because He loves us and wants to give us what we need to do the job He has called us to do.

Jesus has purchased a glorious inheritance for us by the shedding of His blood. As joint-heirs with Him, we can pray boldly.

GOD'S WORD FOR YOU

But you, beloved, build yourselves up [founded] on your most holy faith [make progress, rise like an edifice higher and higher], praying in the Holy Spirit.

JUDE 20

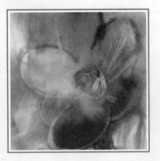

PRAY IN THE SPIRIT

Just as Ephesians 6:18 tells us that we are not only to pray at all times with all manner of prayers, we are also told here by Jude that our prayers are to be "in the Holy Spirit." The apostle Paul tells us in Romans 8:26 that when we don't know how to pray, the Holy Spirit knows how to pray in our weakness.

It is the Holy Spirit of God within us Who provokes us and leads us to pray. Rather than delaying, we need to learn to yield to the leading of the Spirit as soon as we sense it. That is part of learning to pray all manner of prayers at all times, wherever we may be, and whatever we may be doing.

Our motto should be that of the old spiritual song, "Every time I feel the Spirit moving in my heart, I will pray." If we know we can pray anytime and anywhere, we won't feel we have to wait until just the right moment or place to pray.

When we are praying in the Holy Spirit, we can know that our prayers are reaching the throne of God and will be answered.

Ask the Holy Spirit to get involved in everything you do. He is the Helper, and He is waiting for you to ask.

GOD'S WORD FOR YOU

For God did not give us a spirit of timidity (of cowardice, of craven and cringing and fawning fear), but [He has given us a spirit] of power and of love and of calm and well-balanced mind and discipline and self-control.

2 TIMOTHY 1:7

PRAY AND FEAR NOT

God wants us to pray about everything and fear nothing. We could avoid a lot of problems if we would pray more, worry less, and fear less. Timothy says that God has not given us a spirit of fear. So when we feel fear, it is not from God. Any kind of fear—little fear, big fear—is not from God. It's from the devil. And the devil will try to intimidate us with all kinds of fear so that we do not pray.

If Abraham or Joshua or David had bowed their knee to fear when the task before them seemed overwhelming, they never would have experienced God as their abundant provision.

Prayer and God's Word will give you power to overcome fear. Memorize scriptures so when you feel fear, you can open your mouth and confess those scriptures out loud in faith-filled prayer. In fact, I think one of the most important things that we can do in our prayer time is walk around and confess the Word.

So often when we have something that we've got to confront and deal with, we start to dread and fear and wonder and reason what to do. Fear must be confronted. You can't wish fear away. You have to confront it with the Word of God.

Put on the armor of God through prayer and stand against all the enemy's fiery darts of fear.

THE TYPES OF PRAYER

As believers we have spiritual
authority to do God's will
on earth through prayer.

GOD'S WORD FOR YOU

First of all, then, I admonish and urge that petitions, prayers, intercessions, and thanksgivings be offered on behalf of all men,

For kings and all who are in positions of authority or high responsibility, that [outwardly] we may pass a quiet and undisturbed life [and inwardly] a peaceable one in all godliness and reverence and seriousness in every way.

For such [praying] is good and right, and [it is] pleasing and acceptable to God our Savior.

1 TIMOTHY 2:1-3

three

THE TYPES OF PRAYER

od had to teach me some lessons about praying in faith, about understanding that the Holy Spirit was helping me in prayer, and that Jesus was interceding along with me (Romans 8:26; Hebrews 7:25). Two of the Persons of the Godhead are helping me pray!

How often are we to pray? At all times. How are we to pray? In the Spirit, with different kinds of prayer. I believe if we will allow Him to do so, the Holy Spirit will lead us into prayer without ceasing so it becomes like breathing. When that happens we can be continually offering up prayers.

Now I would like to discuss the types of prayer we see in the Word of God. We should be exercising all the various types of prayer on a regular basis. They are simple, can be prayed anywhere at any time, and are most effective when prayed from a believing heart.

God does hear our prayers and does respond to them.
That is what makes them so powerful and so effective.

GOD'S WORD FOR YOU

Again I tell you, if two of you on earth agree (harmonize together, make a symphony together) about whatever [anything and everything] they may ask, it will come to pass and be done for them by My Father in heaven.

MATTHEW 18:19

THE PRAYER OF AGREEMENT

First, let me say that I believe this prayer can only be prayed by two or more people who are committed to living in agreement. This prayer is not for people who generally live in strife and then decide they need to agree for some type of miracle because they are desperate. God honors the prayers of those who pay the price to live in unity.

Because our prayer power multiplies when we are in agreement with those around us (1 Peter 3:7), we need to be in agreement all the time, not just when we face a crisis situation. There will be times in our life when what we are up against is something that is bigger than we are by ourselves. At such times, we will be wise to pray together with someone who is in agreement with us in that situation.

If you feel you have nobody in your life with whom you can agree in prayer, don't despair. You and the Holy Spirit can agree. He is here on the earth with you and in you as a child of God.

There is power in agreement! Pray the prayer of agreement, especially when you feel the need for a little extra prayer power!

GOD'S WORD FOR YOU

Hear my prayer, O Lord, give ear to my supplications! Answer me in Your faithfulness, in Your righteousness!

PSALM 143:1 NASB

Oh, that I might have my request, and that God would grant me the thing that I long for!

JOB 6:8

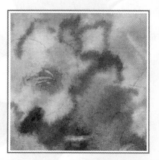

THE PRAYER OF PETITION

This prayer is by far the most often used. When we petition God, we ask for something for ourselves. Another word for petition is *requisition*. It is a demand or request made on something to which a person is legally entitled but not yet in possession of, as in the military when an officer requisitions equipment or supplies for his men. As an officer of the United States Army, he is entitled to that material, but in order to receive it he has to submit a definite request for it.

When we come to the Lord with a petition, we are requisitioning from Him what He has already set aside to provide for us when the need arises. For that reason, we frequently exercise our right to petition God. It is, of course, not wrong to ask God to do things for us, but our petitions should be well-balanced with praise and thanksgiving.

We can be bold in petitioning God for any type of need in our lives. We are not restricted to a certain number of requests per day. We can feel at ease talking to God about anything that concerns us, for He already knows what we need and is willing to grant us our petitions (Matthew 6:8).

When you are in trouble, go to the Throne before you go to the phone.

GOD'S WORD FOR YOU

Speak out to one another in psalms and hymns and spiritual songs, offering praise with voices [and instruments] and making melody with all your heart to the Lord,

At all times and for everything giving thanks in the name of our Lord Jesus Christ to God the Father.

EPHESIANS 5:19-20

Through Him, therefore, let us constantly and at all times offer up to God a sacrifice of praise, which is the fruit of lips that thankfully acknowledge and confess and glorify His name. [Lev. 7:12; Isa. 57:19; Hos. 14:2.]

HEBREWS 13:15

THE PRAYER OF PRAISE AND WORSHIP

Praise is a narration or a tale in which we recount the good qualities about an individual, in this case, God. We should praise the Lord continually. By continually, I mean all throughout the day. We should praise Him for His mighty works, the wonders He has created, and even the works of grace He is yet to do in each of our lives.

A sacrifice of praise means doing it even when we don't feel like it. We should praise God for His goodness, mercy, loving-kindness, grace, long-suffering, and patient nature in the hard times as well as the good. While we are waiting to see the fulfillment of our prayers, we are to be continually offering up to God the fruit of lips that thankfully acknowledge and confess and glorify His name.

It is not our responsibility to worry and fret or try to play God by taking into our own hands situations that should be left to Him alone. Instead, it is our responsibility to cast our care upon the Lord, trusting Him, praying without worry, avoiding works of the flesh, continuing in obedience, bearing good fruit, and offering Him the sacrifice of praise.

May a sacrifice of praise continually be in our mouths for the marvelous works of grace He has done for us.

GOD'S WORD FOR YOU

Thank [God] in everything [no matter what the circumstances may be, be thankful and give thanks], for this is the will of God for you [who are] in Christ Jesus [the Revealer and Mediator of that will].

1 THESSALONIANS 5:18

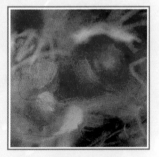

THE PRAYER OF THANKSGIVING

After telling us to pray without ceasing, the apostle Paul directs us to give thanks to God in everything, no matter what our circumstances may be, stating that this is the will of God for us.

Just as prayer is to be a lifestyle for us, so thanksgiving is to be a lifestyle for us. Giving thanks to God should not be something we do once a day as we sit down somewhere and try to think of all the good things He has done for us and merely say, "Thanks, Lord."

That is empty religion, something we do simply because we think God requires it. True thanksgiving flows continually out of a heart that is full of gratitude and praise to God for Who He is as much as for what He does. It is not something that is done to meet a requirement, win favor, gain a victory, or qualify for a blessing.

The type of thanksgiving that God the Father desires is that which is provoked by the presence of His Holy Spirit within us Who moves upon us to express to the Lord verbally what we are feeling and experiencing spiritually.

We are to be thankful to God always, continually acknowledging, confessing, and glorifying His name in prayerful praise and worship.

GOD'S WORD FOR YOU

And I sought a man among them who should build up the wall and stand in the gap before Me for the land, that I should not destroy it, but I found none.

EZEKIEL 22:30

Therefore He is able also to save to the uttermost (completely, perfectly, finally, and for all time and eternity) those who come to God through Him, since He is always living to make petition to God and intercede with Him and intervene for them.

HEBREWS 7:25

THE JOY OF BELIEVING PRAYER

THE PRAYER OF INTERCESSION

To intercede means to *stand in the gap* for someone else, to plead his case before the throne of God. If there is a breach in people's relationship with God due to a particular sin in their life, we have the privilege of placing ourselves in that breach and praying for them. We can intercede for them and expect to see them comforted and encouraged while they wait. We can also expect a timely breakthrough for them concerning their need being met.

I don't know what I would do if people did not intercede for me. I petition God to give me people to intercede for me and for the fulfillment of the ministry to which He has called me. We need each other's prayers of intercession.

Praying for others is equivalent to sowing seed. We must sow seed if we are to reap a harvest (Galatians 6:7). Sowing seed into the lives of other people through intercession is one sure way to reap a harvest in our own life. Each time we pray for someone else, we are inviting God to not only work in that person's life but also in our own.

Intercession is one of the most important ways we carry on the ministry of Jesus Christ that He began in this earth.

We can release God's power in the lives of others by praying for them.

GOD'S WORD FOR YOU

Commit your way to the Lord [roll and repose each care of your load on Him]; trust (lean on, rely on, and be confident) also in Him and He will bring it to pass.

PSALM 37:5

∞

Casting the whole of your care [all your anxieties, all your worries, all your concerns, once and for all] on Him, for He cares for you affectionately and cares about you watchfully.

1 PETER 5:7

∞

THE PRAYER OF COMMITMENT

When we are tempted to worry or take the care of some situation in life, we should pray the prayer of commitment. God intervenes in our situations when we commit them to Him.

In my own life I found that the more I tried to take care of things myself, the bigger mess my life became. I was quite independent and found it difficult to humble myself and admit that I needed help. However, when I finally submitted to God in these areas and found the joy of casting all my care on Him, I could not believe I had lived so long under such huge amounts of pressure.

Commit to the Lord your children, your marriage, your personal relationships, and especially anything you may be tempted to be concerned about. In order to succeed at being ourselves, we must continually be committing ourselves to God, giving to Him those things that appear to be holding us back. Only God really knows what needs to be done, and He is the *only* One Who is qualified to do it. The more we sincerely commit ourselves to Him, the more progress we make.

A believer who can trust the Father when things do not seem to make sense is a mature believer.

GOD'S WORD FOR YOU

I appeal to you therefore, brethren, and beg of you in view of [all] the mercies of God, to make a decisive dedication of your bodies [presenting all your members and faculties] as a living sacrifice, holy (devoted, consecrated) and well pleasing to God, which is your reasonable (rational, intelligent) service and spiritual worship.

ROMANS 12:1

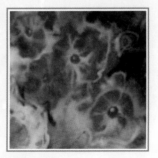

THE PRAYER OF CONSECRATION

Another life-changing type of prayer is the prayer of consecration, the prayer in which we give ourselves to God. In the prayer of consecration, we dedicate our lives and all that we are to Him.

In order for God to use us, we must give ourselves totally to Him. When we truly consecrate ourselves to the Lord, we relinquish the burden of trying to run our own lives. Consecration is a powerful act, but it must be sincere. It is quite easy to sing along with everyone else a song such as "I Surrender All." We may even feel moved emotionally, but the real test is found in daily life when circumstances don't always go the way we thought they would. Then we must sing again, "I Surrender All," consecrating ourselves to God afresh.

Consecration to God is the most important aspect of succeeding at being ourselves. We don't even know what we are supposed to be, let alone know how to become whatever it is. But as we regularly keep our lives on the altar in consecration to God, He will do the work that needs to be done in us so that He may do the work He desires to do *through* us.

When we consecrate ourselves to God,
He makes us into vessels fit for the Master's use.

GOD'S WORD FOR YOU

. . . the Lord is in His holy temple; let all the earth hush and keep silence before Him.

HABAKKUK 2:20

❦

Our inner selves wait [earnestly] for the Lord; He is our Help and our Shield.

PSALM 33:20

❦

THE PRAYER OF SILENCE

I also call this kind of prayer "waiting on the Lord." In our instant and fast-paced society, this spiritual discipline is often lacking. We want it and we want it right now! If we are always in such a hurry, we will miss out on the wisdom God wants to speak to our hearts if we will only be silent before Him.

Elijah was a man who learned the secret of silent, waiting prayer in His presence. After slaying the prophets of Baal, Elijah learned a valuable lesson on waiting on God. The Lord told Elijah to go stand on a mount and wait. A great wind came; then came a great earthquake and a great fire, but the Lord was in none of those. "After the fire [a sound of gentle stillness and] a still, small voice" (1 Kings 19:12).

David also learned to wait in the house of the Lord and "to meditate, consider, and inquire in His temple" (Psalm 27:4). If we want to learn how to pray effectively, then we are going to have to learn to sit in silence and listen for His Word. Waiting and listening takes our focus off of us and places it on Him, Who is the answer to all our needs.

It is often in silence when the power of God is moving the most mightily. Allow the Holy Spirit to teach you how to wait in His presence.

GOD'S WORD FOR YOU

Now when Jesus went into the region of Caesarea Philippi, He asked His disciples, Who do people say that the Son of Man is?

Simon Peter replied, You are the Christ, the Son of the loving God.

MATTHEW 16:13, 16

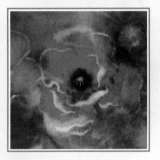

THE PRAYER OF CONFESSION

When Peter made that statement about Jesus being the Christ, the Son of the living God, he was releasing with his mouth the faith that was in his heart. The praying and confession of what we know in our hearts, revealed by the Holy Spirit, is a powerful way to pray and strengthen our faith.

We must understand that we establish the faith that is in our heart by the words we speak from our mouth, as the apostle Paul tells us in Romans 10:10: "... and with the mouth he confesses (declares openly and speaks out freely his faith) and confirms [his] salvation."

That is why prayer is so important. Because we establish the things we believe inwardly when we start talking about them outwardly. That is why confessing the Scriptures in prayer is also very powerful. When we do that, we are establishing things in the spiritual realm by the words we are speaking in the physical realm. And eventually what is established spiritually will be manifested physically.

You and I should be constantly confessing the Word of God, believing in our heart and confessing with our mouth what God has said about us in His Word.

We release heaven's power when we confess in the physical realm what God has already done for us in the spiritual realm

GOD'S WORD FOR YOU

Rejoice in the Lord always [delight, gladden yourselves in Him]; again I say, Rejoice!

PHILIPPIANS 4:4

⌖

I will rejoice in You and be in high spirits; I will sing praise to Your name, O Most High!

PSALM 9:2

⌖

THE PRAYER OF REJOICING

Twice in the passage from Philippians the apostle Paul tells us to rejoice. He urges us not to fret or have any anxiety about anything but to pray and give thanks to God *in* everything—not *after* everything is over.

If we wait until everything is perfect before rejoicing and giving thanks, we won't have much fun. Learning to enjoy life even in the midst of trying circumstances is one way we develop spiritual maturity. Paul also writes that we "are constantly being transfigured into His very own image in ever increasing splendor and from one degree of glory to another" (2 Corinthians 3:18). We need to learn how to enjoy the glory we are experiencing at each level of our development. Let's learn to pray a prayer of rejoicing and be glad in the Lord this day and every day along the way toward our goal.

When I first started my ministry, I depended on my circumstances for happiness. Finally the Lord showed me the doorway to happiness. He gave me a breakthrough by teaching me that fullness of joy is found in His *presence*—not in His *presents*! (Psalm 16:11.)

True joy comes from seeking God's face.

WHY
PRAYER ISN'T
ANSWERED

There's no power shortage in heaven,
but there is often a shortage
of prayers on earth.

GOD'S WORD FOR YOU

And, beloved, if our consciences (our hearts) do not accuse us [if they do not make us feel guilty and condemn us], we have confidence (complete assurance and boldness) before God,

And we receive from Him whatever we ask, because we [watchfully] obey His orders [observe His suggestions and injunctions, follow His plan for us] and [habitually] practice what is pleasing to Him.

1 JOHN 3:21-22

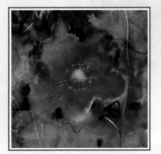

four
WHY PRAYER ISN'T ANSWERED

 f there's anything I want to know for sure, it's that my prayers are going to be answered when I go to prayer. For a long time I was frustrated that I didn't see my prayers answered the way I would have liked. I knew that I had a loving heavenly Father Who delights in answering our petitions. But something wasn't working, so I sought the Lord. He began to instruct me in His Word about a number of obstacles that will hinder our prayer life. As I began to line up my life with the issues He showed me, I began to see more faith and power in my prayer life. And more answers to my prayers!

When you go to pray, do you feel uncomfortable? Maybe you're under condemnation, maybe you're not praying as a righteous person, or maybe you're regarding iniquity in your heart.

If we are going to get our prayers answered, then we are going to have to learn how to tap into the spiritual realm and allow the Holy Spirit to show us what obstacles He wants to remove from our lives. Then we must be obedient to what He shows us so that our prayers become fervent and effective for the Kingdom of God.

❧

Allow the Holy Spirit to convict, cleanse, and fill you so that your prayers are filled with faith and power.

GOD'S WORD FOR YOU

And when that time comes, you will ask nothing of Me [you will need to ask Me no questions]. I assure you, most solemnly I tell you, that My Father will grant you whatever you ask in My Name [as presenting all that I AM]. [Exod. 3:14.]

Up to this time you have not asked a [single] thing in My Name [as presenting all that I AM]; but now ask and keep on asking and you will receive, so that your joy (gladness, delight) may be full and complete.

JOHN 16:23-24

PEOPLE DON'T PRAY BOLDLY

Our prayers aren't answered because we don't pray boldly. We need to pray more specifically and have the boldness to come before God and really ask Him for what we want and not be ashamed to make our requests known.

One of the major things that keeps people from praying boldly is they look at what they have done wrong instead of what Jesus has done right. The Bible teaches us plainly that God ". . . made Christ [virtually] to be sin Who knew no sin, so that in and through Him we might become [endued with, viewed as being in, and examples of] the righteousness of God" (2 Corinthians 5:21). Because we are righteous in Him, we can approach the throne of grace boldly with our needs (Hebrews 4:16).

John 16:23-24 tells us we can come boldly before the throne in Jesus' name. The name of Jesus is powerful. When I use Jesus' name in my prayers, it's not like some magic charm that I tack on to the end of everything. When I go in the name of Jesus, I'm saying, "Father, I come to you presenting today all that Jesus is—not what I am."

Don't be vague—be bold! You'll be surprised at the answers you'll get.

God loves to answer our bold prayers made in the name of Jesus.

GOD'S WORD FOR YOU

If I regard iniquity in my heart, the Lord will not hear me. [Prov. 15:29; 28:9; Isa. 1:15; John 9:31; James 4:3.]

PSALM 66:18

We know that God does not listen to sinners; but if anyone is God-fearing and a worshiper of Him and does His will, He listens to him.

JOHN 9:31

Iniquity in My Heart

Our prayers often do not get answered because we regard iniquity in our heart. David said, "If I regard iniquity in my heart, the Lord will not hear me" (Psalm 66:18). What that means, to put it bluntly, is that the Lord doesn't hear us when we pray if we come before Him with unclean hearts.

If there is sin your life, you will not be able to pray boldly or with confidence. When you're praying and you sense that you're not comfortable, stop and ask God why. Ask Him to reveal anything that's hidden. If He convicts you of something, don't be vague about it. Call it what it is—sin. We get release when we admit and confess our sin and bring it out in the open. He wants you to confess it so He can cleanse you and restore a clean conscience so that you can pray (1 John 1:9). There is power in truth and honesty when we come clean before the Lord and walk in the light.

Make sure your heart is clean before Him so your prayers are alive and energized by the Holy Spirit's power.

God hears your prayers
when you approach Him with a clean heart.

GOD'S WORD FOR YOU

For this reason we also, from the day we heard of it, have not ceased to pray and make [special] request for you, [asking] that you may be filled with the full (deep and clear) knowledge of His will in all spiritual wisdom [in comprehensive insight into the ways and purposes of God] and in understanding and discernment of spiritual things. . . .

COLOSSIANS 1:9

PEOPLE DON'T PRAY IN THE WILL OF GOD

Another reason why prayer is not answered is that people don't pray in the will of God. I'd like to say we're all led by the Spirit, and we all hear the voice of God. That's the place we're working toward, but we're not all there yet.

Sometimes it's not all that easy to decipher if what you're wanting is really God's will or just your flesh wanting it. In order to know God's will, you must know God's Word. Psalm 119:105 says, "Your word is a lamp to my feet and a light to my path." We must become students of the Word. Another issue comes into play regarding God's will: God's timing. To be out of God's timing is also to be out of His will. If I try to make it happen right now, then it's out of the will of God for today for my life.

First John 5:14 says, "and this is the confidence (the assurance, the privilege of boldness)." If I'm not praying in the will of God, He is not going to hook up with me and give me the power to pray with that boldness. But if you know the will of God concerning your prayer request, then faith will come out of your spirit to help you pray.

*It's amazing what faith can do
when we know the will of God.*

GOD'S WORD FOR YOU

. . . You do not have, because you do not ask. [I John 5:15.]

[Or] you do ask [God for them] and yet fail to receive, because you ask with wrong purpose and evil, selfish motives.

JAMES 4:2-3

WRONG PURPOSE AND MOTIVES

According to James 3:3, many prayers are not answered because people pray amiss. To pray amiss means we are praying with the "wrong purpose and evil, selfish motives." You could be praying for something that is the will of God, but you're praying for the wrong reason. When you first start to learn to pray, you're carnal, so you are going to pray carnally. You're going to pray many prayers for the wrong reason. We're not talking about what we do but why we're doing it.

Years ago I spent many hours praying for my ministry to grow. I wanted to look good in front of everybody, and I wanted to look successful. I wanted it to appear that I was obviously hearing from God. And I wanted those people to come to my meetings because the more people came, the better I looked.

Now I know who I am in Christ, and I know that my worth is not in my ministry. Back then I was praying with the wrong motive. Do you want your prayer life to be powerful and effective? Then before you go to prayer start checking your motives. Make sure you are praying for godly reasons with all humility.

When God finds humility and right motives,
His grace empowers our prayers.

GOD'S WORD FOR YOU

Truly I tell you, whoever says to this mountain, Be lifted up and thrown into the sea! and does not doubt at all in his heart but believes that what he says will take place, it will be done for him.

MARK 11:23

If any of you is deficient in wisdom, let him ask of the giving God [Who gives] to everyone liberally and ungrudgingly, without reproaching or faultfinding, and it will be given him.

Only it must be in faith that he asks with no wavering (no hesitating, no doubting). For the one who wavers (hesitates, doubts) is like the billowing surge out at sea that is blown hither and thither and tossed by the wind.

JAMES 1:5-6

DOUBT AND UNBELIEF

Another reason why prayer is not answered is that people have doubt and unbelief in their hearts. Doubt brings in confusion and often depression. It kills our faith and causes us to make negative confessions.

In Luke 18, Jesus told His disciples a parable to the effect that they ought always to pray and not to turn coward, faint, lose heart, and give up. He spoke of the widow who continued to plead her case before the unjust judge until he acted on her behalf. Jesus is saying that if an unjust judge can be moved by persistence, how much more will our loving heavenly Father be moved if we won't quit and give up because of doubt and unbelief.

We need to learn to move in the realm of the Spirit through faith, instead of relying on what we see in the natural. "For we walk by faith . . . not by sight or appearance" (2 Corinthians 5:7). Learn to stay in contact with God, always walking in His presence. If you begin to listen to the devil's lies, then soon doubt and unbelief come roaring back. Those fiery darts begin to wage war with your mind. Remember that doubt and unbelief are a product of the mind and our wrong focus.

Looking unto Jesus, the Author and Finisher of our faith, will stop doubt and unbelief.

GOD'S WORD FOR YOU

Enter into His gates with thanksgiving and a thank offering and into His courts with praise! Be thankful and say so to Him, bless and affectionately praise His name!

PSALM 100:4

I will give You thanks in the great assembly; I will praise You among a mighty throng.

PSALM 35:18

INGRATITUDE

Prayer is often not answered because people are ungrateful. There are people who are grumblers, murmurers, faultfinders, and complainers. We have to be very careful that we're not like that. We need to be the kind of people who are thankful for what God is doing. If we are complaining and ungrateful all the time, we are going to have a hard time getting answers to our prayers.

If you want to see God work in your spouse, your children, your finances, your circumstances, or your job, you have to be grateful for what you already have.

God told me once, "Joyce, when people are praying and asking Me for things, if they don't have a thankful heart, that's a clear indication to Me that they're already grumbling trying to handle what they have." The devil's whole plan is to keep you dissatisfied with something all the time, grumbling, faultfinding, and complaining. When you are ungrateful, it holds you back from progressing and maturing in the Spirit.

God wants us to grow in maturity and become more like His Son Jesus. God's answer to ingratitude is a life filled with praise and thanksgiving.

Look for something today to be thankful for and offer up a prayer of praise and thanksgiving.

GOD'S WORD FOR YOU

*So shall My word be that goes forth out of My mouth;
it shall not return to Me void [without producing any
effect, useless], but it shall accomplish that which I please
and purpose, and it shall prosper in the thing for which I
sent it.*

ISAIAH 55:11

∞

*For the Word that God speaks is alive and full of
power [making it active, operative, energizing, and
effective]; it is sharper than any two-edged sword,
penetrating to the dividing line of the breath of life (soul)
and [the immortal] spirit, and of joints and marrow [of the
deepest parts of our nature], exposing and sifting and
analyzing and judging the very thoughts and purposes of
the heart.*

HEBREWS 4:12

∞

PRAYERS NOT BASED ON THE WORD

We also fail to get answers to our prayers because they are not based on the Word of God. The prophet Isaiah says, "My word . . . shall not return to Me void." God says that His Word will always accomplish the purpose for which He has sent it. Learn the Word, speak the Word, pray the Word. Let God know that you are standing on the foundation of the Word.

When the devil tries to lie to you, quote him the Scriptures. The Bible says that the Word is "sharper than any two-edged sword" (Hebrews 4:12). We need to make sure that our prayers are prayers being produced by the Spirit of God and not our soulish prayers. If we stay in the Word, God will teach us when we're operating in the soul and when we're operating in the Spirit. The Holy Spirit uses the Word to judge the very thoughts and purposes of our hearts.

If I'm speaking God's Word in line with His will, then I can be assured that what I'm praying for will not come back empty-handed. God promises to fulfill His Word.

The Holy Spirit will quicken the Word to you to empower your prayers with faith and assurance.

GOD'S WORD FOR YOU

Death and life are in the power of the tongue, and they who indulge in it shall eat the fruit of it [for death or life]. [Matt. 12:37.]

PROVERBS 18:21

He who guards his mouth keeps his life, but he who opens wide his lips comes to ruin.

PROVERBS 13:3

NEGATIVE CONFESSION

If we want our prayers to be answered, we can't pray and then negate them with a negative confession. Let's say a mother is praying for a son who's having trouble in school. So she prays the prayer of faith and believes God for a breakthrough. Then she goes to lunch with two neighbors and spends the next hour saying, "I am so sick of these problems I'm having with this kid. Why me?"

This kind of negative confession wipes your prayer slate clean. You might as well not even waste your time praying until you make a decision to get your mouth in line with your prayers.

When the neighbors ask how your son is doing, say, "You know what? In the natural things have not changed a whole lot, but I'm praying for him, and I have assurance in my heart that God is doing a mighty work in his life."

Once you have laid hold of the answer through faith, then you need to make sure your confession is in agreement with what you've asked God to do. Don't let the devil trip you up when people ask you questions that you could answer negatively. Answer them with a positive confession of the Word of God.

When you line up your mouth
with the positive confession of the Word of God,
you'll see amazing results.

GOD'S WORD FOR YOU

And the servant of the Lord must not strive.

2 TIMOTHY 2:24 KJV

Let all bitterness and indignation and wrath (passion, rage, bad temper) and resentment (anger, animosity) and quarreling (brawling, clamor, contention) and slander (evil-speaking, abusive or blasphemous language) be banished from you, with all malice (spite, ill will, or baseness of any kind).

EPHESIANS 4:31

TRIFE

Strife is a thief and a robber that we must learn to recognize and deal with quickly. We must control strife before it controls us.

Strife is defined as "the act or state of fighting or quarreling, especially bitterly . . . discord." It is bickering, arguing, being involved in a heated disagreement, or shows up as an angry undercurrent. Strife is dangerous. It is a demonic force sent by Satan for the purpose of destruction.

Almost any time someone hurts us, or offends us, anger rises up within us. It is not sin to feel anger. But we must not act out the angry feelings in an ungodly way. We must not hold a grudge or get into bitterness, resentment, or unforgiveness.

A judgmental attitude is an open door for strife. We must remember that mercy triumphs over judgment (James 2:13 NIV). Judgment usually leads to gossip. Gossip begins to spread the strife from person to person. It gets us out of agreement, harmony, and unity. It actually moves us out of God's blessings.

When the temptation comes to judge others, and then spread our opinion through gossip and backbiting, we should remember this helpful hint: Let the one among us who is without sin cast the first stone (John 8:7).

Remember: God changes things through prayer and faith, not through judgment and gossip.

GOD'S WORD FOR YOU

And whenever you stand praying, if you have anything against anyone, forgive him and let it drop (leave it, let it go), in order that your Father Who is in heaven may also forgive you your [own] failings and shortcomings and let them drop.

But if you do not forgive, neither will your Father in heaven forgive your failings and shortcomings.

MARK 11:25-26

Then Peter came up to Him and said, Lord, how many times may my brother sin against me and I forgive him and let it go? [As many as] up to seven times?

Jesus answered him, I tell you, not up to seven times, but seventy times seven! [Gen. 4:24.]

MATTHEW 18:21-22

*U*NFORGIVENESS

One of the greatest reasons why prayer isn't answered among Christians is *unforgiveness*. In Mark 11 Jesus gave His disciples a command to forgive. And then He told them plainly that if they did not forgive, neither would their Father in heaven forgive them their failings and shortcomings. He was blunt with them because He knew what a stumbling block unforgiveness would be for their spiritual life.

It is important to note that forgiveness and having faith to move mountains comes in the same context. There is no power in speaking to a mountain if the heart is full of unforgiveness. Yet this problem is rampant among God's children. If there is anything that will short-circuit God from answering our prayers, it's a heart full of unforgiveness and bitterness toward others. You can't go into your prayer closet and expect God to move mountains for you or on behalf of others when you've hardened your heart with unforgiveness.

Jesus told Peter that he must be willing to forgive seven times seventy: 490 times. Jesus wanted to show His disciples that forgiveness was one of the main keys for unlocking the Kingdom of God in their lives if they wanted to have power in their prayers.

✤

Extend abundant mercy and forgiveness
just as God forgave you in Christ.

PRAYER IN JESUS' NAME

*We have been given the most powerful
Name in heaven and earth
to use when we pray. Let's use it!*

GOD'S WORD FOR YOU

And [so that you can know and understand] what is the immeasurable and unlimited and surpassing greatness of His power in and for us who believe, as demonstrated in the working of His mighty strength,

Which He exerted in Christ when He raised Him from the dead and seated Him at His [own] right hand in the heavenly [places],

Far above all rule and authority and power and dominion and every name that is named [above every title that can be conferred], not only in this age and in this world, but also in the age and the world which are to come.

And He has put all things under His feet and has appointed Him the universal and supreme Head of the church [a headship exercised throughout the church], [Ps. 8:6.]

Which is His body, the fullness of Him Who fills all in all [for in that body lives the full measure of Him Who makes everything complete, and Who fills everything everywhere with Himself].

EPHESIANS 1:19-23

five

PRAYER IN JESUS' NAME

 used the name of Jesus for many years without the results I had been told I could have. I began asking God why I was using the name that was supposed to have power over circumstances that were outside His will, and yet I was not seeing results. The Holy Spirit began to reveal to me that releasing the power in the name of Jesus requires faith in that name, that name that is so powerful that when it is mentioned in faith, every knee must bow in three realms—in heaven, on earth, and under the earth!

Jesus came from the highest heaven; He has been to the earth, and He has descended to Hades, under the earth, and now is seated again at the right hand of the Father in the highest heaven. He has made a full circle; therefore, He has filled everything and everywhere with Himself. He is seated above everything else and has a name above every other name. His name is the highest name, the most powerful name—and His name has been given to us to use in prayer!

What an awesome privilege we have to use the name of Jesus that is above every other name!

GOD'S WORD FOR YOU

A woman, when she gives birth to a child, has grief (anguish, agony) because her time has come. But when she has delivered the child, she no longer remembers her pain (trouble, anguish) because she is so glad that a man (a child, a human being) has been born into the world.

So for the present you are also in sorrow (in distress and depressed); but I will see you again and [then] your hearts will rejoice, and no one can take from you your joy (gladness, delight).

And when that time comes, you will ask nothing of Me [you will need to ask Me no questions]. I assure you, most solemnly I tell you, that My Father will grant you whatever you ask in My Name [as presenting all that I AM]. [Exod. 3:14.]

Up to this time you have not asked a [single] thing in My Name [as presenting all that I AM]; but now ask and keep on asking and you will receive, so that your joy (gladness, delight) may be full and complete.

JOHN 16:21-24

His NAME TAKES HIS PLACE

Oh, how wonderful it would have been to have physically walked with Jesus. But He told His followers they would be better off when He went away, because then He would send His Spirit to dwell in every believer (John 16:7).

He told them that even though they were sorrowful at the news of His upcoming departure, they would rejoice again just as a woman has sorrow during her labor but rejoices when the child is born.

He said they would change their minds when they saw the glory of His Spirit in them and the power available to each of them through the privilege of using His name in prayer. He was literally giving to them—and has given to all those who believe in Him—His "power of attorney," the legal right to use His name. His name takes His place; His name represents Him.

Jesus has already been perfect for us. He has already pleased the Father for us; therefore, there is no pressure on us to feel that we must have a perfect record of right behavior before we can pray. Then when we come before the Father in Jesus' name, we can confess our sin, receive His forgiveness, and boldly make our requests known to Him.

When the name of Jesus is spoken by a believer in faith, all of heaven comes to attention.

GOD'S WORD FOR YOU

If ye shall ask any thing in my name, I will do it.

JOHN 14:14 KJV

∞

Then some of the traveling Jewish exorcists (men who adjure evil spirits) also undertook to call the name of the Lord Jesus over those who had evil spirits, saying, I solemnly implore and charge you by the Jesus Whom Paul preaches!

Seven sons of a certain Jewish chief named Sceva were doing this.

But [one] evil spirit retorted, Jesus I know, and Paul I know about, but who are you?

Then the man in whom the evil spirit dwelt leaped upon them, mastering two of them, and was so violent against them that they dashed out of that house [in fear], stripped naked and wounded.

ACTS 19:13-16

∞

THE JOY OF BELIEVING PRAYER

ᴊ*ESUS*' NAME IS NOT MAGIC

The name of Jesus is not a "magic word" or a ritualistic incantation to be added to the end of a prayer to insure its effectiveness.

In the Book of Acts we read of the mighty miracles that God did through the life of Paul. God honored Paul's faith when he spoke the name of Jesus. Certain Jewish exorcists, however, attempted to use the name of Jesus as if it were a simple incantation to be said. The Bible says the "man in whom the evil spirit dwelt leaped upon them, mastering two of them" (Acts 19:16). The spirit spoke and said it knew Jesus and Paul but not them.

If we are going to pray and use the powerful name of Jesus, then we must be in a living, obedient relationship with Him. Then the power of the Holy Spirit will flow out of our lives and deliver us and others from the devil's bondages.

All Spirit-led prayer involves praying the will of God, not the will of man! It is impossible to pray the will of God without knowing the Word of God. Yes, God certainly pays attention to the prayers that come to Him in Jesus' name, but not ones that are outside of His will.

❧

You must know Jesus as Lord
before you can use His name in power.

109

GOD'S WORD FOR YOU

Behold! I have given you authority and power to trample upon serpents and scorpions, and [physical and mental strength and ability] over all the power that the enemy [possesses]; and nothing shall in any way harm you.

LUKE 10:19

And His name, through and by faith in His name, has made this man whom you see and recognize well and strong.

ACTS 3:16

THE NAME OF JESUS IS POWER

The name of Jesus is power. No loving parent would release power to a baby, because the parent knows the child would get hurt. Parents don't withhold power from their children to hurt them, but to help them or to keep them safe. Our heavenly Father is the same way. He tells us what is available to us, and then by His Spirit helps us mature to the point where we can handle what He desires to give us.

I believe the power in the name of Jesus is unlimited. I also believe that our heavenly Father releases it to us as He knows we can handle it properly.

When Jesus began to talk to His disciples about the privilege of praying in His name and having their requests granted, He said, "I *solemnly* tell you . . ." I believe that the power of God is a solemn responsibility. God's power is not a toy! It is not to be released to people who are only playing, but to those who are seriously ready to get on with God's program for their lives.

As you continue to grow and mature in Christ, you can look for exciting new dimensions in your walk with the Lord.

GOD'S WORD FOR YOU

And it shall be that whoever shall call upon the name of the Lord [invoking, adoring, and worshiping the Lord—Christ] shall be saved.

ACTS 2:21

IN TIMES OF CRISIS

Years ago before seatbelt laws, a friend of mine was driving with his young son through a busy intersection one day. The car door on the passenger side was not secured tightly, and he made a sharp turn. The car door flew open, and the little boy rolled out right into traffic! The last thing my friend saw was a set of car wheels just about on top of his son. All he knew to do was cry, "Jesus!"

He stopped his car and ran to his son. To his amazement, his son was perfectly all right. But the man driving the car that had almost hit the child was hysterical.

"Man, don't be upset!" my friend said. "My son is okay. Just thank God you were able to stop!"

"You don't understand!" the man responded. "I never touched my brakes!"

Although there was nothing man could do, the name of Jesus prevailed, and the boy's life was spared.

In times of crisis, call upon the name of Jesus. The more you and I see how faithful He is in times of need and crises, the more we witness the power in His name over situations and circumstances, the more our faith is developed in His name.

There is power in the name of Jesus for every crisis we will ever face.

GOD'S WORD FOR YOU

Let this same attitude and purpose and [humble] mind be in you which was in Christ Jesus: [Let Him be your example in humility:]

Who, although being essentially one with God and in the form of God [possessing the fullness of the attributes which make God God], did not think this equality with God was a thing to be eagerly grasped or retained,

But stripped Himself [of all privileges and rightful dignity], so as to assume the guise of a servant (slave), in that He became like men and was born a human being,

And after He had appeared in human form, He abased and humbled Himself [still further] and carried His obedience to the extreme of death, even the death of the cross!

Therefore [because He stooped so low] God has highly exalted Him and has freely bestowed on Him the name that is above every name.

PHILIPPIANS 2:5-8

OBEDIENCE AND THE NAME OF JESUS

Jesus became extremely obedient; therefore, He was given a name that is above every other name. But let's not get so caught up in the power these verses set forth that we forget the obedience they describe.

John 14:15 says: "If you [really] love Me, you will keep (obey) My commands."

Obedience is important!

Now I realize that the ability is not in us (apart from the Lord's help) to be perfectly obedient, but if we have a willing heart within us, and if we do what we can do, then He will send His Spirit to do what we cannot do.

I am not suggesting that the power in Jesus' name won't work without perfect obedience. I am making a point that the power in the name of Jesus will not be released to anyone who is not seriously pressing toward the mark of the high calling in Christ (Philippians 3:14 KJV), which is maturity—and maturity requires extreme obedience. Extreme obedience requires a willingness to suffer in the flesh, in a godly way, for example, by denying yourself something you want that you know isn't good for you, if need be, in order to know and do the will of God.

In order for us to experience the freedom Jesus purchased for us, we need to be obedient to His Word.

GOD'S WORD FOR YOU

For [instance] a married woman is bound by law to her husband as long as he lives; but if her husband dies, she is loosed and discharged from the law concerning her husband.

Likewise, my brethren, you have undergone death as to the Law through the [crucified] body of Christ, so that now you may belong to Another, to Him Who was raised from the dead in order that we may bear fruit for God.

ROMANS 7:2, 4

But the person who is united to the Lord becomes one spirit with Him.

1 CORINTHIANS 6:17

To Use the Name, You Must Be "Married"!

I was studying about the name of Jesus when the Lord spoke to my heart. He said, "Joyce, when you married Dave, you got his name and the power of all the name Meyer means." He reminded me that I can use the name Dave Meyer and get the same results that Dave could get himself if he were with me. I can even go to the bank and get Dave Meyer's money, because when two people get married, all the property of each now belongs to the other.

Through this example of everyday life, the Holy Spirit was attempting to teach me that although I had a relationship with the Lord, it was more like a courtship than a marriage. I liked "to go on dates" with Him, but when "the date" was over, I wanted to go my own way. I wanted all of Him and His favor and benefits, but I did not want to give Him all of myself.

The apostle Paul tells us that we have died to the law of sin and death and are now married to Another so that we can bear fruit for Him. Remember, you cannot legally use the name until after the marriage to Jesus.

*Jesus is the Bridegroom, and we are His Bride.
That is how God the Father has planned it,
and that is the only way His plan will work properly.*

GOD'S WORD FOR YOU

Then Jesus called together the Twelve [apostles] and gave them power and authority over all demons, and to cure diseases,

And He sent them out to announce and preach the kingdom of God and to bring healing.

LUKE 9:1-2

EXERCISING AUTHORITY IN THE NAME

As believers we need to recognize that the power of attorney gives the right to *command* in Jesus' name.

We pray and ask the Father for things in Jesus' name, but we command the enemy in that name. We speak to circumstances and principalities and powers, using the authority that has been given us by virtue of the power of attorney invested in us by Jesus Himself. In exercising our deliverance ministry, we don't lay hands on a person and begin to pray for God to cast it out. We command it to come out in the name of Jesus.

Before we can exercise this authority, we have already prayed to the Father in Jesus' name. Now we go and use the power He has granted us, and we exercise the authority inherent in the name of His Son Jesus.

The same thing applies to healing the sick. There are times to pray the prayer of faith in the name of Jesus (James 5:15); there are times to anoint with oil (James 5:14); but there are also times simply to command or speak in the name of Jesus.

Spend time daily with the Lord. Fellowship, ask, pray, seek, and come out of that time equipped for the job at hand.

When you go to do the work of the Kingdom, exercise your authority in Jesus' name.

GOD'S WORD FOR YOU

But Peter said, Silver and gold (money) I do not have; but what I do have, that I give to you: in [the use of] the name of Jesus Christ of Nazareth, walk!

ACTS 3:6

DO NOT BE SELFISH WITH THE NAME

I believe there are those who have heard messages about the power that is available to them in the name of Jesus, and who are busy using that name hoping to get everything they have ever wanted. We certainly can and should use the name in our own behalf, as long as we use it to fulfill God's will for our life and not our own. However, there is another aspect of using the name in prayer: *using the name of Jesus to pray for others*.

That is really what the apostles were doing in the book of Acts. Jesus had sent them out empowered with His authority and His name, and they got busy trying to help others with it. They were using the name of Jesus to bring salvation, healing, deliverance, and the baptism of the Holy Spirit to all those for whom Jesus had died who did not yet know Him.

Take the name of Jesus and love people with it. When you see a need, whisper a prayer in Jesus' name. God has entrusted every believer with two ministries: the ministry of *reconciliation* and the ministry of *intercession*.

So much can be accomplished in the earth as believers begin to use the name of Jesus unselfishly.

GOD'S WORD FOR YOU

Now to Him Who, by (in consequence of) the [action of His] power that is at work within us, is able to [carry out His purpose and] do superabundantly, far over and above all that we [dare] ask or think [infinitely beyond our highest prayers, desires, thoughts, hopes, or dreams].

EPHESIANS 3:20

EXCEEDINGLY, ABUNDANTLY ABOVE AND BEYOND

When I pray about all the people who are hurting, I have a strong desire to help them all. I feel that my desire is bigger than my ability, and it is—but it is not bigger than God's ability!

When the thing we are facing in our life or ministry looms so big in our eyes that our mind goes "tilt," we need to *think in the spirit*. In the natural, many things are impossible. But God wants us to believe for great things, make big plans, and expect Him to do things so great it leaves us with our mouths hanging open in awe.

God does not usually call people who are capable; if He did, He would not get the glory. He frequently chooses those who, in the natural, feel as if they are in completely over their heads but who are ready to stand up on the inside and take bold steps of faith. They have learned the secret of using Jesus' name and depending on that "superabundant" power that works within them.

When our desires seem overwhelmingly big, and we don't see the way to accomplish them, we should remember that even though we don't know the way, we know the Waymaker!

Because of His abundant power within us, God has a way for us to do everything He places in our heart.

GOD'S WORD FOR YOU

And Moses said to God, Behold, when I come to the Israelites and say to them, The God of your fathers has sent me to you, and they say to me, What is His name? What shall I say to them?

And God said to Moses, I AM WHO I AM and WHAT I AM, and I WILL BE WHAT I WILL BE; and He said, You shall say this to the Israelites, I AM has sent me to you!

EXODUS 3:13-14

◦❈◦

Jesus replied, I assure you, most solemnly I tell you, before Abraham was born, I AM.

JOHN 8:58

◦❈◦

THE NAME OF GOD IS I AM

I have pondered these verses for a long time. To me, they are awesome scriptures that hold much more than we may realize. What was God saying to Moses when He referred to Himself as I AM?

God is saying He is so much, so great, that there is no way to describe Him properly. How can we describe in one name Someone Who is everything? God said to Moses, "I AM can take care of anything you encounter. Whatever you need, I AM it. Either I have it or I can get it. If it doesn't exist, I will create it. I have everything covered, not only now, but for all time. Relax!"

Jesus responded to His disciples the same way God the Father responded to Moses. Revelation 1:8 declares Jesus to be the Alpha and the Omega. That means the first and the last, the beginning and the end. He has always been and always will be.

Our finite human minds cannot expand far enough even to begin to comprehend the limitless power that has been invested in His glorious name.

When we pray in the name of Jesus, we are praying in the name of the great I AM—the omnipotent God of all eternity.

The Lord is the Ever-Present I AM. Always with us. Everything we need, or ever will need.

THE HARRISON HOUSE VISION

Proclaiming the truth and the power
Of the Gospel of Jesus Christ
With Excellence;

Challenging Christians to
Live victoriously,
Grow spiritually,
Know God intimately.

JOYCE MEYER

Joyce Meyer has been teaching the Word of God since 1976 and in full-time ministry since 1980. Joyce's Life In The Word radio broadcasts are heard across the country, and her television broadcasts are seen around the world. She travels extensively, sharing her life-changing messages in Life In The Word conferences and in local churches.

Joyce and her husband, Dave, are the parents of four children. They make their home in St. Louis, Missouri.

Additional copies of this book are available from your local bookstore.

If this book has changed your life, we would like to hear from you.

Please write us at:

📖 Harrison House Publishers
P. O. Box 35035 • Tulsa, OK 74153
www.harrisonhouse.com

To contact the author, write:
Joyce Meyer Ministries
P. O. Box 655 • Fenton, Missouri 63026

or call: (636) 349-0303

Internet Address: www.joycemeyer.org

In Canada, write: Joyce Meyer Ministries Canada, Inc.
Lambeth Box 1300 • London, ON N6P 1T5

or call: (636) 349-0303

In Australia, write: Joyce Meyer Ministries-Australia
Locked Bag 77 • Mansfield Delivery Centre
Queensland 4122

or call: (07) 3349 1200

In England, write: Joyce Meyer Ministries
P. O. Box 1549 • Windsor • SL4 1GT
or call: 01753 831102